T0071633

rinet

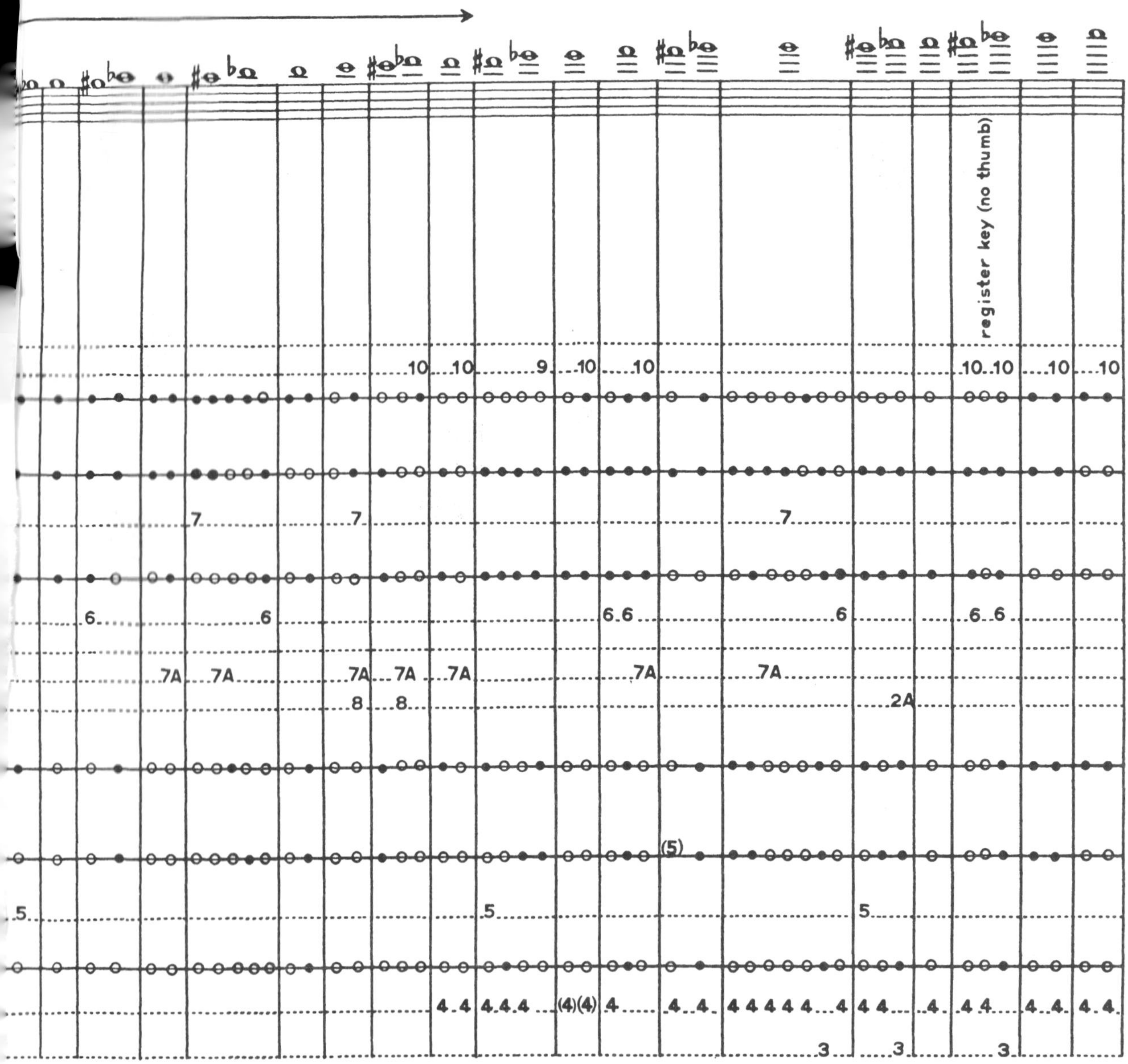

register key (no thumb)

10 10 9 10 10 10 10 10 10

7 7 7

6 6 6 6 6 6 6

7A 7A 7A 7A 7A 7A 7A

8 8 2A

(5)

5 5 5

4 4 4 4 4 4 (4) (4) 4 4 4 4 4 4 4 4 4 4 4 4 4 4 4 4 4 4 4

3 3 3

lf
le

RUBANK EDUCATIONAL LIBRARY No. 157

REVISED EDITION

CLARINET

Vol. II

H. VOXMAN
AND
WM. GOWER

AN OUTLINED COURSE OF STUDY
DESIGNED TO FOLLOW UP ANY
OF THE VARIOUS ELEMENTARY
AND INTERMEDIATE METHODS

NOTE

THE RUBANK ADVANCED METHOD for Clarinet is published in two volumes, the course of study being divided in the following manner:

Vol. I — Keys of C, F, G, B♭, and D Major. Keys of A, D, E, G, and B Minor.

Vol. II — Keys of E♭, A, A♭, E, D♭, and B Major. Keys of C, F♯, F, and C♯ Minor.

PREFACE

THIS METHOD is designed to follow any of the various Elementary and Intermediate instruction series, or Elementary instruction series comprising two or more volumes, depending upon the previous development of the student. The authors have found it necessary in their teaching experience to draw from many sources in order to provide a progressive course of study. The present publication assembles in two volumes, the material essential to a well-rounded musical development.

THE OUTLINES, one of which is included in each of the respective volumes, tend to afford an objective picture of the student's progress. They will facilitate the ranking of members in a large ensemble or they may serve as a basis for awards of merit. In addition, a one-sided development along strictly technical or strictly melodic lines is avoided. The use of these outlines, however, is not imperative and they may be discarded at the discretion of the teacher.

H. Voxman — Wm. Gower

OUTLINE
OF
RUBANK ADVANCED METHOD
FOR
CLARINET, Vol. II
BY
H. Voxman and Wm. Gower

UNIT	SCALES and ARPEGGIOS	(Key)	MELODIC INTERPRETATION	ARTICULATION	FINGER EXERCISES	ORNAMENTS	SOLOS	UNIT COMPLETED
1	5 (1) 6 (5)	E♭	21 (1)	49 (1)	58 (1) (2)	62 (1)	72 (1)	
2	5 (2) 6 (6)	E♭	22 (2)	49 (2)	58 (3) (4)	62 (2)	72 (1)	
3	5 (3) 6 (7)	E♭	23 (3)	50 (3)	58 (5) (6)	62 (3)	72 (1)	
4	6 (4) (8)	E♭	23 (3)	50 (3)	58 (7) (8)	62 (3)	72 (1)	
5	7 (9) (10)	c	26 (4)	50 (4)	58 (9) (10)	63 (4)	72 (1)	
6	7 (11) (12)	c	27 (5)	51 (5)	58 (11)	63 (5)	72 (1)	
7	7 (13) (14)	c	27 (5)	51 (5)	58 (12)	63 (6)	74 (2)	
8	8 (15) 9 (19)	A	28 (6)	51 (6)	58 (13)	64 (7)	74 (2)	
9	8 (16) 9 (20)	A	29 (7)	51 (7)	58 (14)	64 (8)	74 (2)	
10	8 (17) 9 (21)	A	30 (8)	52 (8)	58 (15) (16)	64 (8)	75 (3)	
11	8 (18)	A	30 (8)	52 (8)	58 (17)	65 (9)	75 (3)	
12	9 (22) 10 (25)	f#	31 (9)	52 (9)	58 (18)	65 (10)	75 (3)	
13	10 (23) (26)	f#	32 (10)	52 (10)	58 (19) (20)	65 (11)	75 (3)	
14	10 (24) (27) (28)	f#	32 (10)	52 (10)	58 (21)	66 (12ABC)	75 (3)	
15	11 (29) 12 (33)	A♭	33 (11)	53 (11)	58 (22)	66 (13)	75 (3)	
16	11 (30) 12 (34)	A♭	34 (12)	53 (12)	58 (23)	66 (13)	76 (4)	
17	11 (31) 12 (35)	A♭	36 (13)	53 (13)	58 (24)	67 (14)	76 (4)	
18	12 (32) (36)	A♭	36 (13)	53 (13)	58 (25) (26)	67 (15)	76 (4)	
19	13 (37) (38)	f	37 (14)	54 (14)	58 (27)	67 (16)	76 (4)	
20	13 (39) 14 (40)	f	38 (15)	54 (15)	58 (28)	67 (17)	77 (5)	
21	14 (41) (42)	f	38 (15)	54 (15)	58 (29)	68 (18)	77 (5)	
22	14 (43) 15 (47)	E	38 (16)	54 (16)	58 (30)	68 (18)	77 (5)	
23	14 (44) 15 (48)	E	38 (16)	55 (17)	58 (31) (32) (33)	68 (19)	77 (5)	
24	15 (45) 16 (49)	E	40 (17)	55 (18)	59 (34) (35) (36)	69 (20)	77 (5)	
25	15 (46) 16 (50)	E	40 (17)	55 (18)	59 (37)	69 (21)	78 (6)	
26	16 (51) (52)	c#	42 (18)	55 (19)	59 (38) (39) (40)	69 (21)	78 (6)	
27	16 (53) 17 (54)	c#	42 (18)	56 (20)	59 (41) (42) (43)	70 (22)	78 (6)	
28	17 (55) (56)	c#	44 (19)	56 (20)	59 (44) (45) (46)	70 (22)	78 (6)	
29	17 (57) (58)	D♭	45 (20)	56 (21)	59 (47)	70 (23)	78 (6)	
30	17 (59) 18 (62)	D♭	45 (20)	56 (21)	59 (48) (49)	70 (23)	78 (6)	
31	18 (60) (63)	D♭	46 (21)	57 (22)	59 (50) (51) (52)	70 (24)	79 (7)	
32	18 (61) 19 (64) (65)	D♭	46 (21)	57 (22)	59 (53) (54)	70 (24)	79 (7)	
33	19 (66) 20 (70)	B	47 (22)	57 (23)	59 (55) (56) (57)	70 (25)	79 (7)	
34	19 (67) 20 (71)	B	47 (22)	57 (23)	59 (58) (59) (60)	70 (25)	79 (7)	
35	19 (68) 20 (72)	B	48 (23)	57 (24)	59 (61) (62)	71 (26)	79 (7)	
36	20 (69)	B	48 (23)	57 (24)	59 (63) (64)	71 (26)	79 (7)	

NUMERALS designate page number.
ENCIRCLED NUMERALS designate exercise number.
COMPLETED EXERCISES may be indicated by crossing out the rings, thus, 

PRACTICE AND GRADE REPORT

FIRST SEMESTER

Student's Name ____________________ Date __________

Week	Sun.	Mon.	Tue.	Wed.	Thu.	Fri.	Sat.	Total	Parent's Signature	Grade
1										
2										
3										
4										
5										
6										
7										
8										
9										
10										
11										
12										
13										
14										
15										
16										
17										
18										
19										
20										

Semester Grade ______

Instructor's Signature ____________________

SECOND SEMESTER

Student's Name ____________________ Date __________

Week	Sun.	Mon.	Tue.	Wed.	Thu.	Fri.	Sat.	Total	Parent's Signature	Grade
1										
2										
3										
4										
5										
6										
7										
8										
9										
10										
11										
12										
13										
14										
15										
16										
17										
18										
19										
20										

Semester Grade ______

Instructor's Signature ____________________

Scales and Arpeggios

E♭ Major

TR refers to thumb and register key throughout this book.

Copyright MCMLIII by Rubank, Inc., Chicago, Ill.
International Copyright Secured

4
simile
Chromatic Scale
5
Scale in Thirds
6
Common Chord
7
Dominant 7th Chord
8

C Minor

Natural
Harmonic
9
Melodic
10
Chromatic Scale
11
Scale in Thirds
12
Common Chord
13
Diminished 7th Chord
14

A Major

Scale in Thirds
19
Common Chord
20
Dominant 7th Chord
8va ad lib.
21
F# Minor
Natural
Harmonic
22
Melodic

8va ad lib. (Use chromatic F♯s where applicable)
23
simile
simile
24
simile
Chromatic Scale
25
Scale in Thirds
8va ad lib.
26
Common Chord
8va ad lib.
27
Diminished 7th Chord
28

29
simile
simile
30
simile
31
simile
simile

32
simile
Chromatic Scale
33
Scale in Thirds
34
Common Chord
35
Dominant 7th Chord
36

F Minor

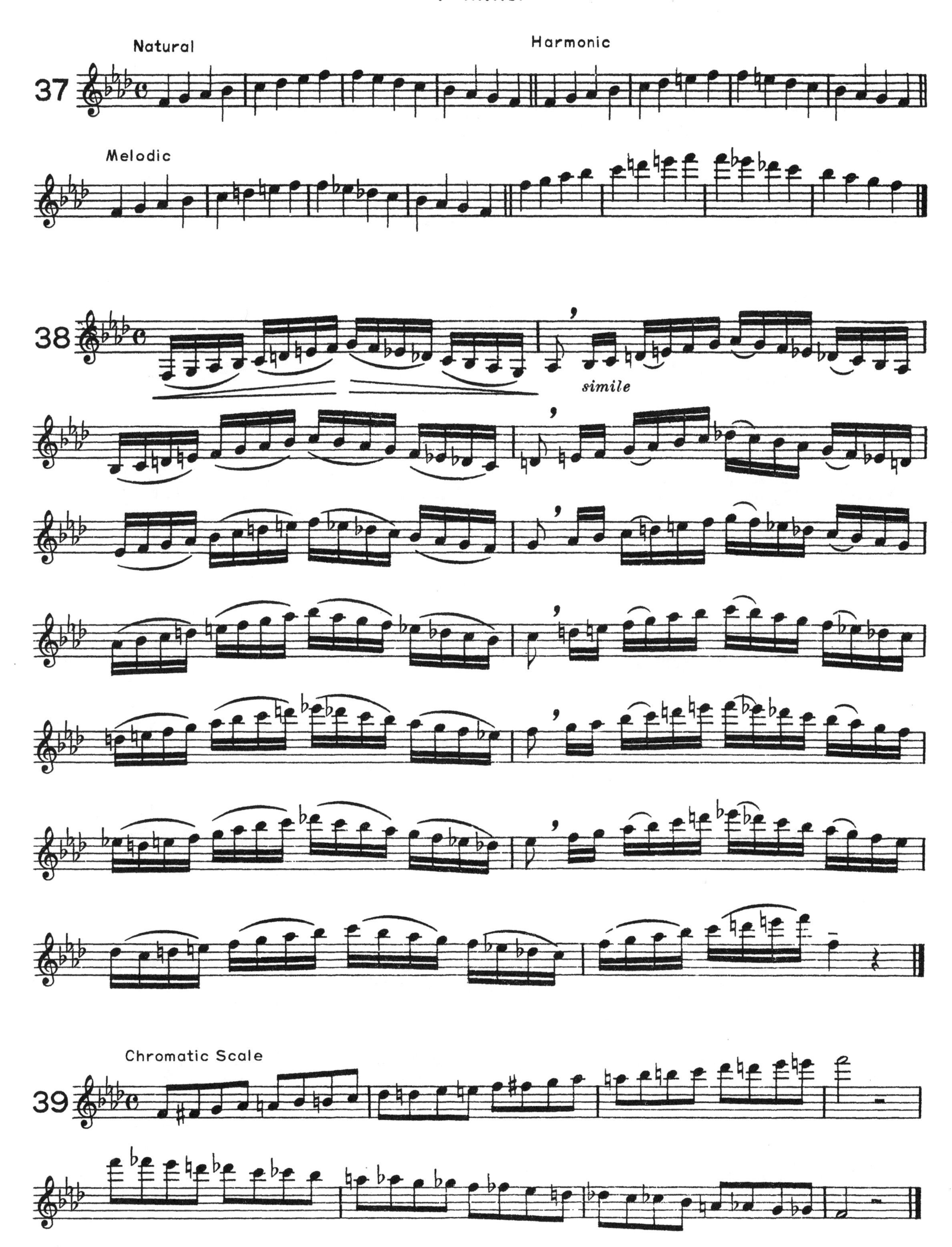

Scale in Thirds
40
Common Chord
41
Diminished 7th Chord
Also practice 8va lower
42
E Major
43
simile
44
simile
simile

45
simile
46
Chromatic Scale
Also practice 8va
47
Scale in Thirds
Also practice 8va
48

Common Chord
Also practice 8va
49
Dominant 7th Chord
50
C# Minor
Natural
Harmonic
51
Melodic
52
simile
simile
Chromatic Scale
53

Scale in Thirds
54
Common Chord
55
Diminished 7th Chord
56
D♭ Major
(Use chromatic fingerings on G♭s.)
57
simile
58
simile
simile
59
simile
simile

60
simile
simile
61
Chromatic Scale
62
Scale in Thirds
63

Common Chord
64
Dominant 7th Chord
65
B Major
66
simile
simile
67
simile
simile
68
simile

69
simile
Scale in Thirds
70
Common Chord
71
Dominant 7th Chord
Also practice 8va
72

Studies in Melodic Interpretation

For One or Two Part Playing

The following studies have been selected with the idea of ensemble performance in mind. Much effort has been expended in selecting duets in which the first and second parts are melodically and rhythmically independent. Students should be encouraged to practice these numbers as duets outside of the lesson period. When circumstances permit, any number of students can perform them as an ensemble. The lower part of the duets may be assigned at the discretion of the teacher.

Careful attention to the marks of expression is essential to effective use of the material. Where different dynamic signs are written for the upper and lower parts, observe them accurately. The part having the melody must always slightly predominate even when the dynamic indications are the same.

Pencil the technically difficult passages and devote extra time to their mastery.

In rhythmic music in the more rapid tempi (marches, dances, etc.) tones that are equal divisions of the beat are played somewhat detached (staccato). Tones that equal a beat or are multiples of a beat are held full value. Tones followed by rests are usually held full value. This point should be especially observed in slow music.

WANHAL
Allegretto
2
p
dolce
f
p
f
p
dolce
p
cresc.
cresc.
a tempo
p
ritard.
dolce
p
f
f
p
cresc.
p
f
f

Two Minuets

HAYDN

I

f
sf
p
D.C. al Fine
(with repeat)
II
p espressivo
cresc.
decresc.
p dolce
espressivo

p
dolce
cresc.
f
p
dolce
p
p
mf
mf
p
p
f
f
p dolce
cresc.
mf
p
p

MAGNANI

GEMINIANI

AUBERT

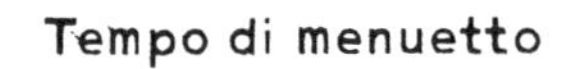

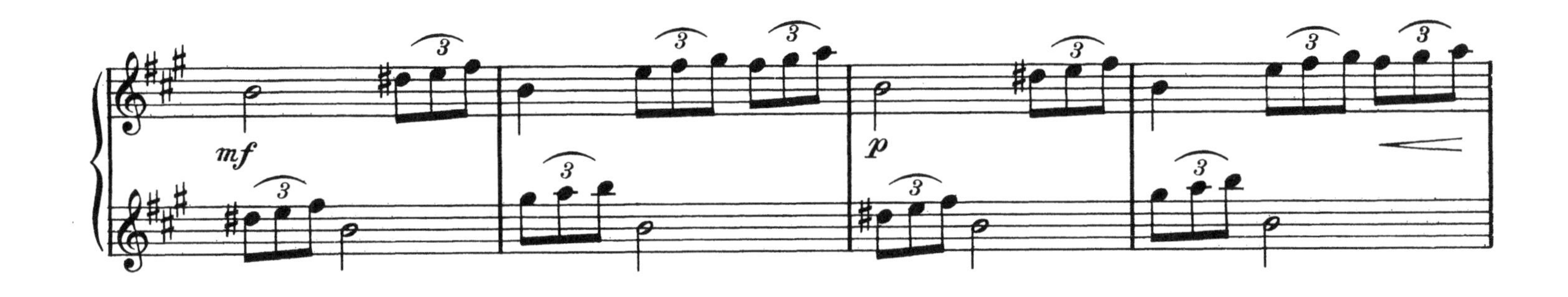

STAMITZ

Andante [In four]
7
p dolce
tr
f
tr
Fine
sotto voce
cresc.
f
p dolce
p dolce
f
f
p
fp
p
f
p
p
D. C. al Fine

PLEYEL
(adapted)
Allegro non troppo
8
p
mf
f
(,)
dim.
p
rit.
a tempo
mf
3

cresc.
cresc.
Allegro
CAMPAGNOLI
9

MAGNANI

Largo assai sostenuto (in 3)
10
pp
pp
con anima
pp
pp
con anima
rall.

GEMINIANI
Largo simplice e sostenuto (in three)
11
p
cresc.
dim.
dolce
dolce
cresc.
mf
dim.
p
cresc.
dolce
cresc.
f
p
p

MAGNANI
Moderato molto sostenuto
12
ppp ed espressivo
più mosso e
animando

rall.
animando come prima
*R
1º Tempo
rit.
dolcissimo espressivo
affrett.
cresc.
ff rit. assai
*R = right hand, little finger.

*R = right hand, little finger.
L = left hand, little finger.

GEMINIANI

Allegro appassionato
14
mf
mf
p
dolce
f
p
f
p
cresc.
f
dolce
f
p
p
f

MAGNANI

Rondo

PLEYEL

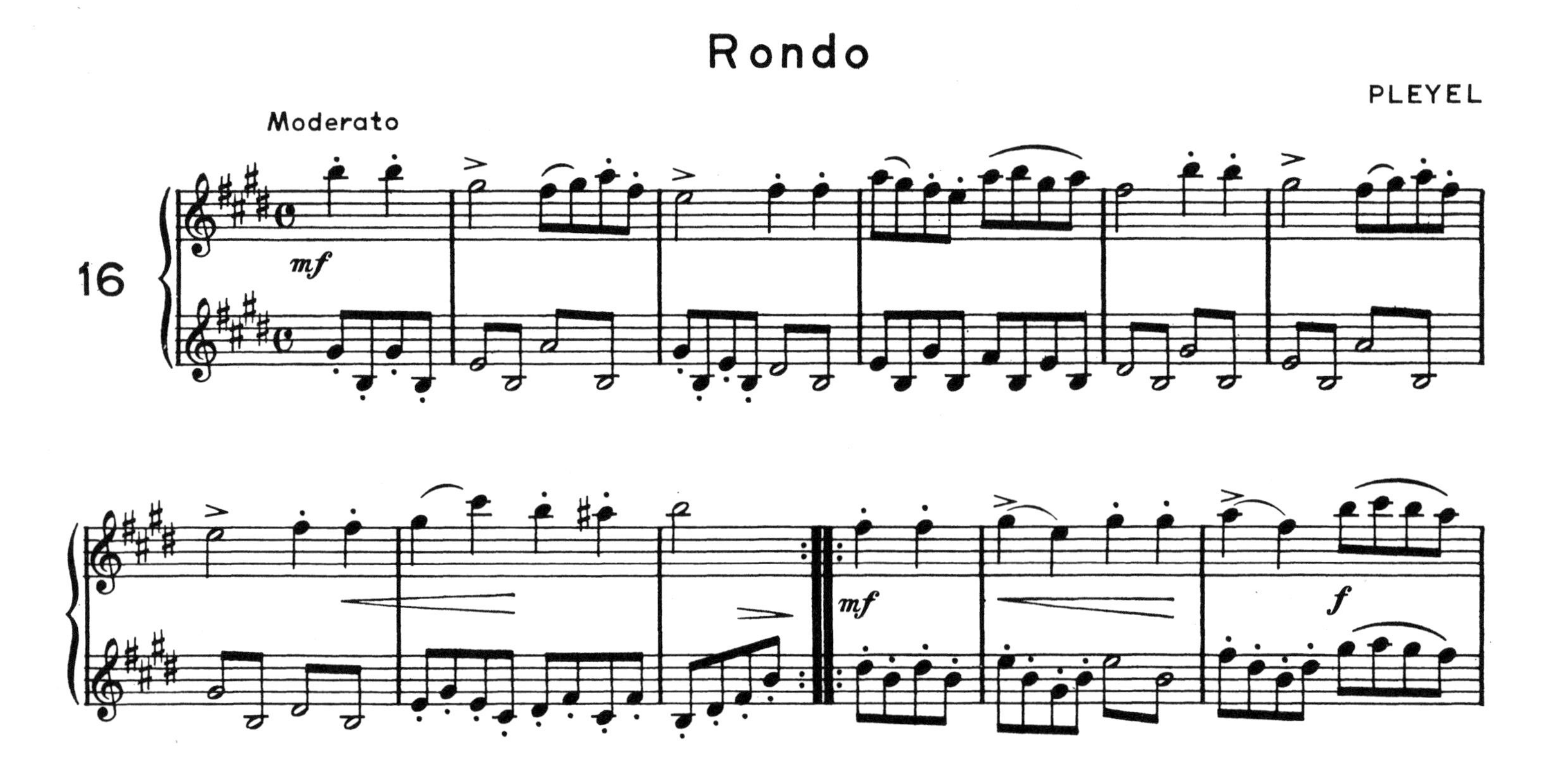

MOZART
17
Adagio
(1)
fp
p
3
1
2
pp
Minuetto
f
(1)

fz
f
p
cresc.
Fine
TRIO
dolce
fp
fz
tr
Minuetto D. C. al Fine

LUFT

fp
rit.
a tempo
marcato
marcato
pp
R
L
mf
p
pp
dim.

SELLNER
Adagio con espressione
19
p
sf
cresc.
f
sf
mp
mf
pp
R
L

Canon
Note the different dynamics of the two melodic lines.
W. F. BACH
Larghetto
20
p
tr
mf
1
2
pp

Gigue

BOISMORTIER

MOZART

GEMINIANI
Andante
23
p
simplice e sostenuto
mf
mf
f
dim.
p
cresc.
cresc.
f
p
cresc.
dim.
p

Studies in Articulation

The material for this section has been taken for the most part from various standard methods for the clarinet and the violin.

Play the exercises as quickly as technic permits unless otherwise indicated.

3
4

5
6
simile
7
simile

Andantino
8
p
f
f
p
9
Moderato
10
f

11
p
p
rit.
12
f
simile
R
13
f

14
15
f
sf
sf
sf
16

17
mf
p
18
p
p
p
f
p
19
simile

Adagio molto espressivo (in four)
20
p
p
f
p
rubato
cresc.
rit.
p
a tempo
p
pp
morendo
21
p
cresc.
f
p
p
p
cresc.
f

Allegretto (in one)
22
Fine
D. C. al Fine
23
Fine
D.C. al Fine
24
simile

Exercises in Fingering

Practice these exercises slowly and increase in rapidity as the difficulties in fingering are overcome.

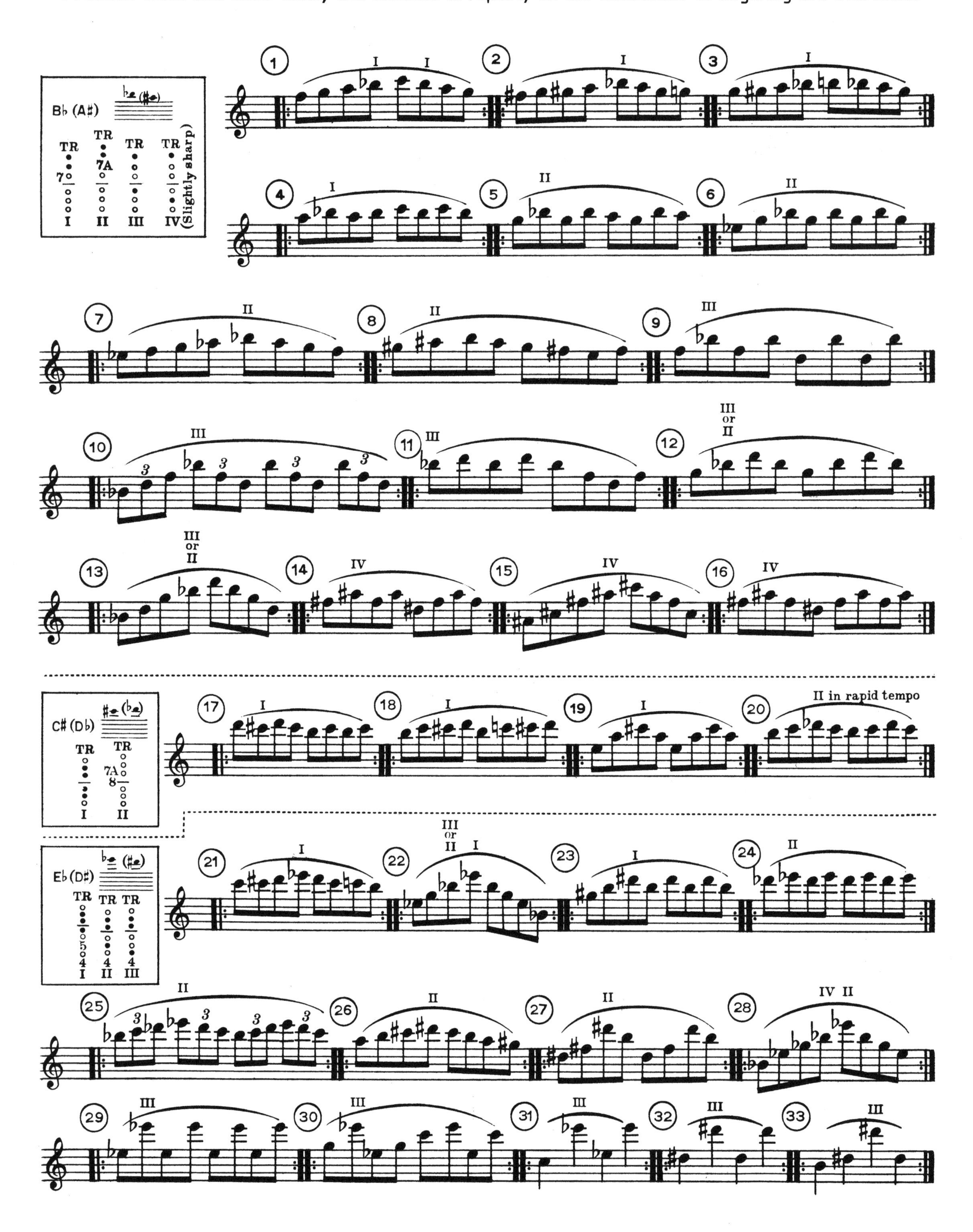

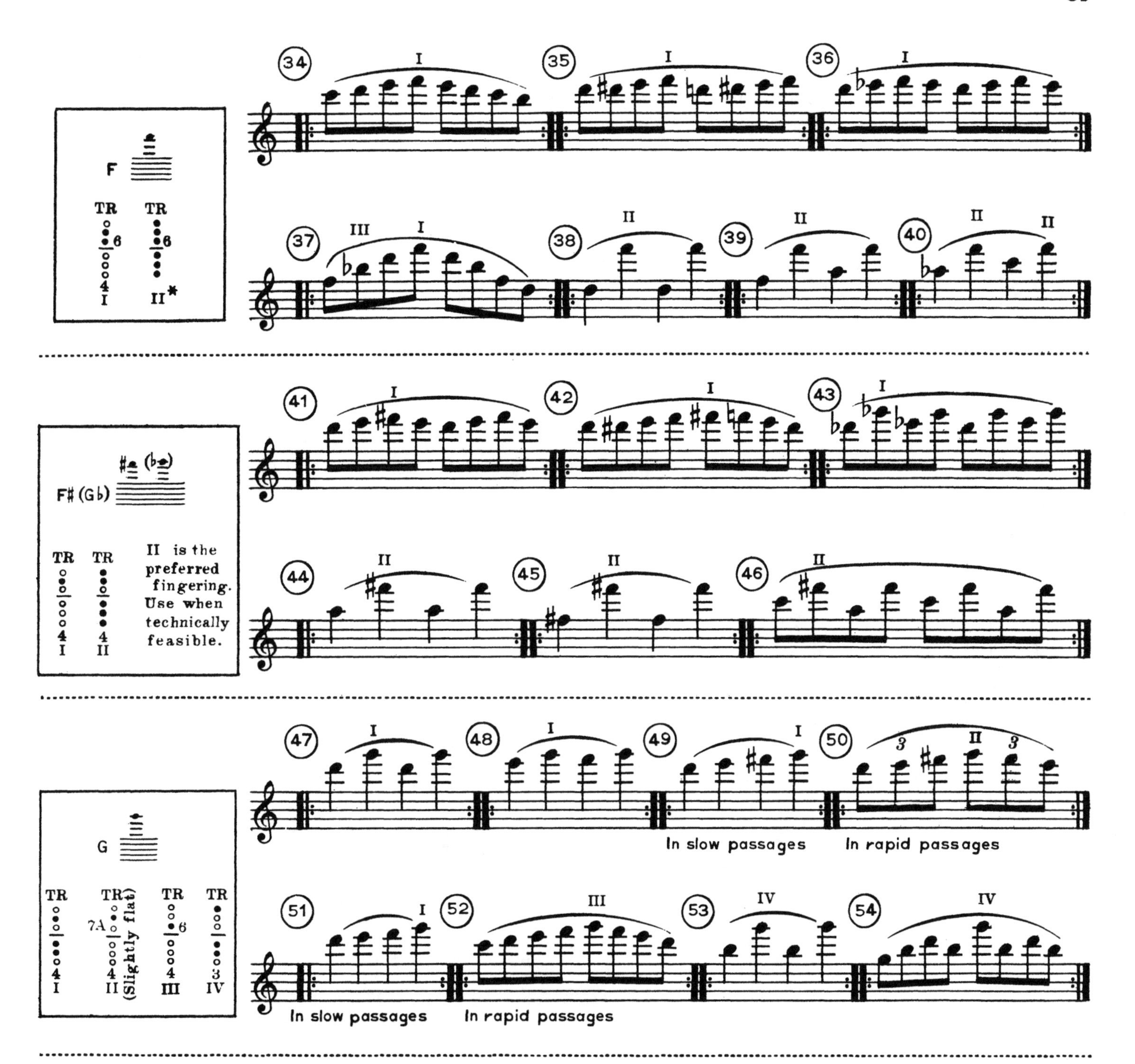

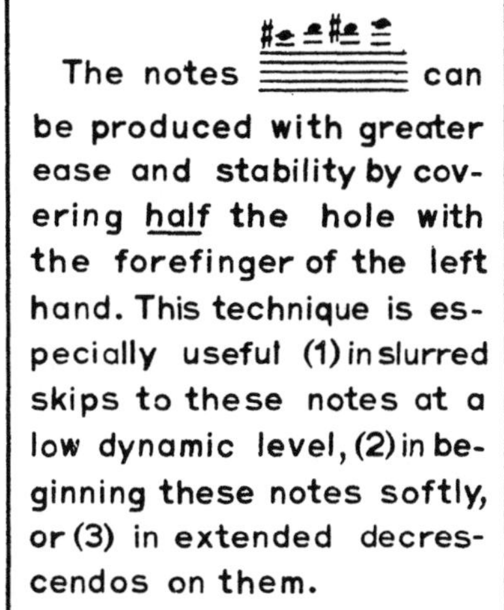

The notes can be produced with greater ease and stability by covering *half* the hole with the forefinger of the left hand. This technique is especially useful (1) in slurred skips to these notes at a low dynamic level, (2) in beginning these notes softly, or (3) in extended decrescendos on them.

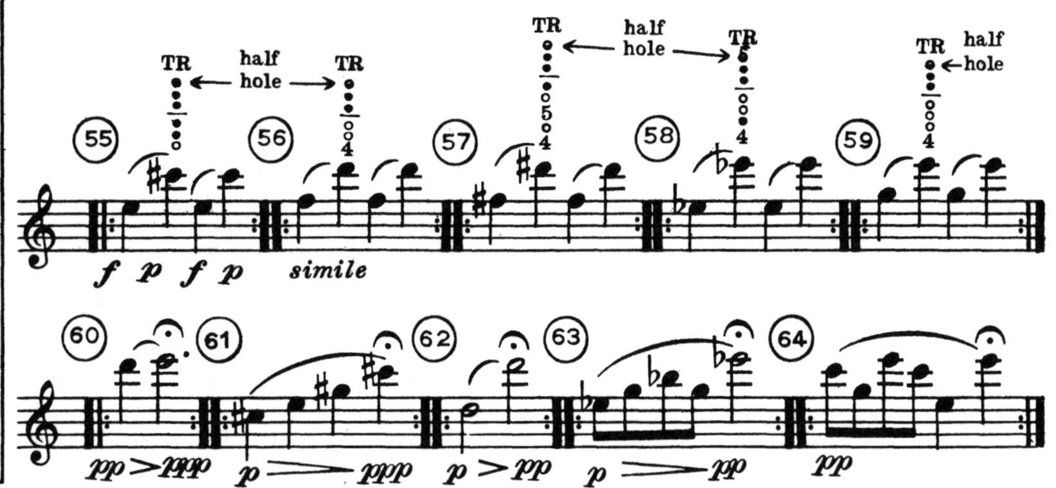

* Not possible on clarinets having the articulated C♯ - G♯

Table of Trills for the Boehm Clarinet (17 Keys–6 Rings)

Trill finger-holes or keys enclosed by ∼ ∼. Use key 12 on all trills from upward.

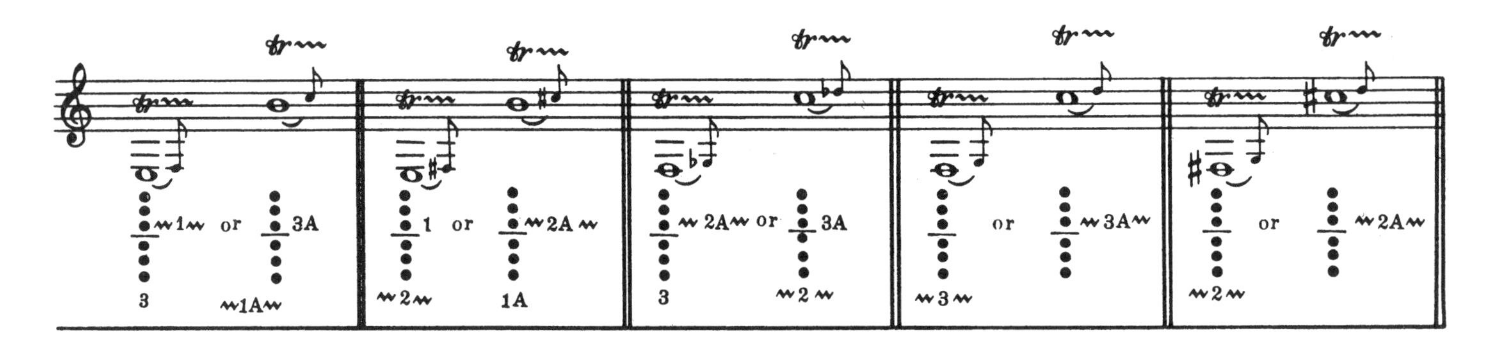

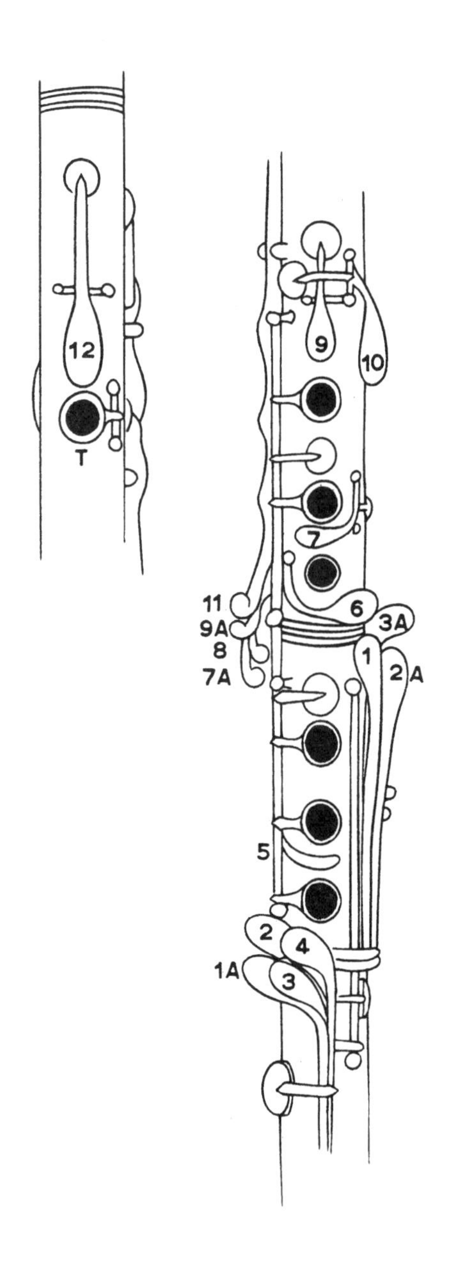

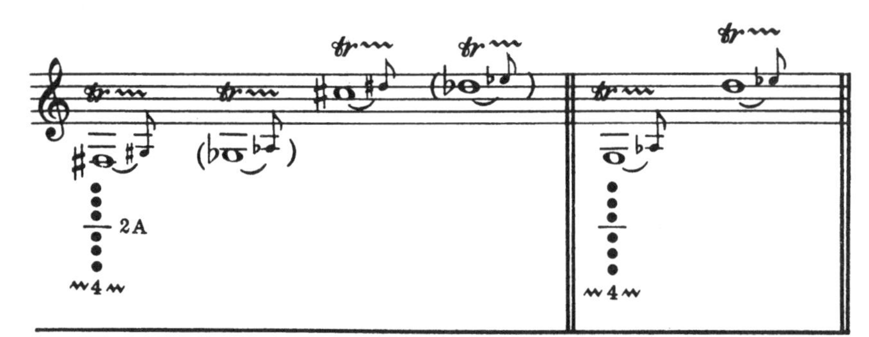

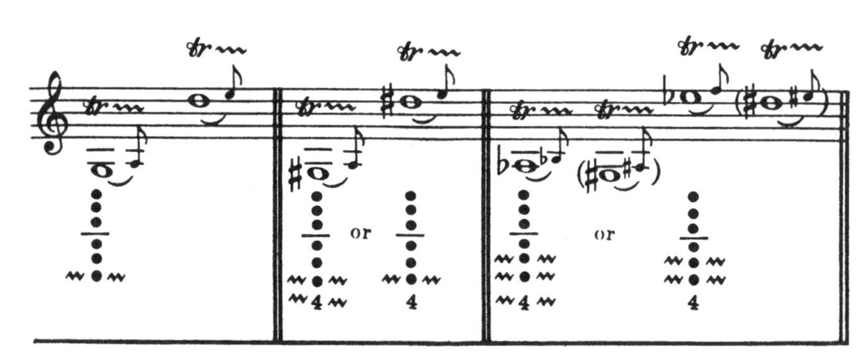

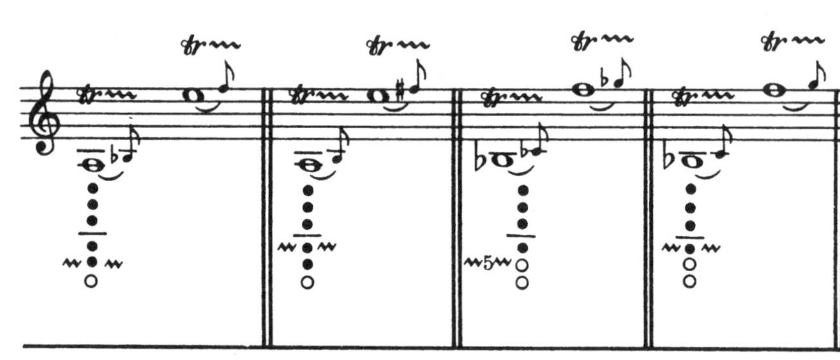

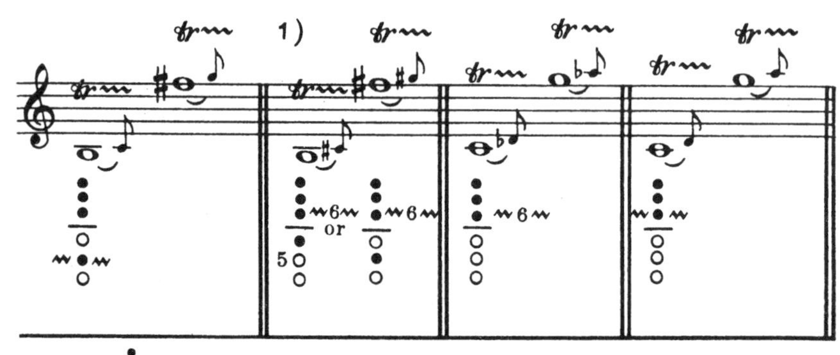

1.) Trill 6 on clarinets with articulated C♯ - G♯.

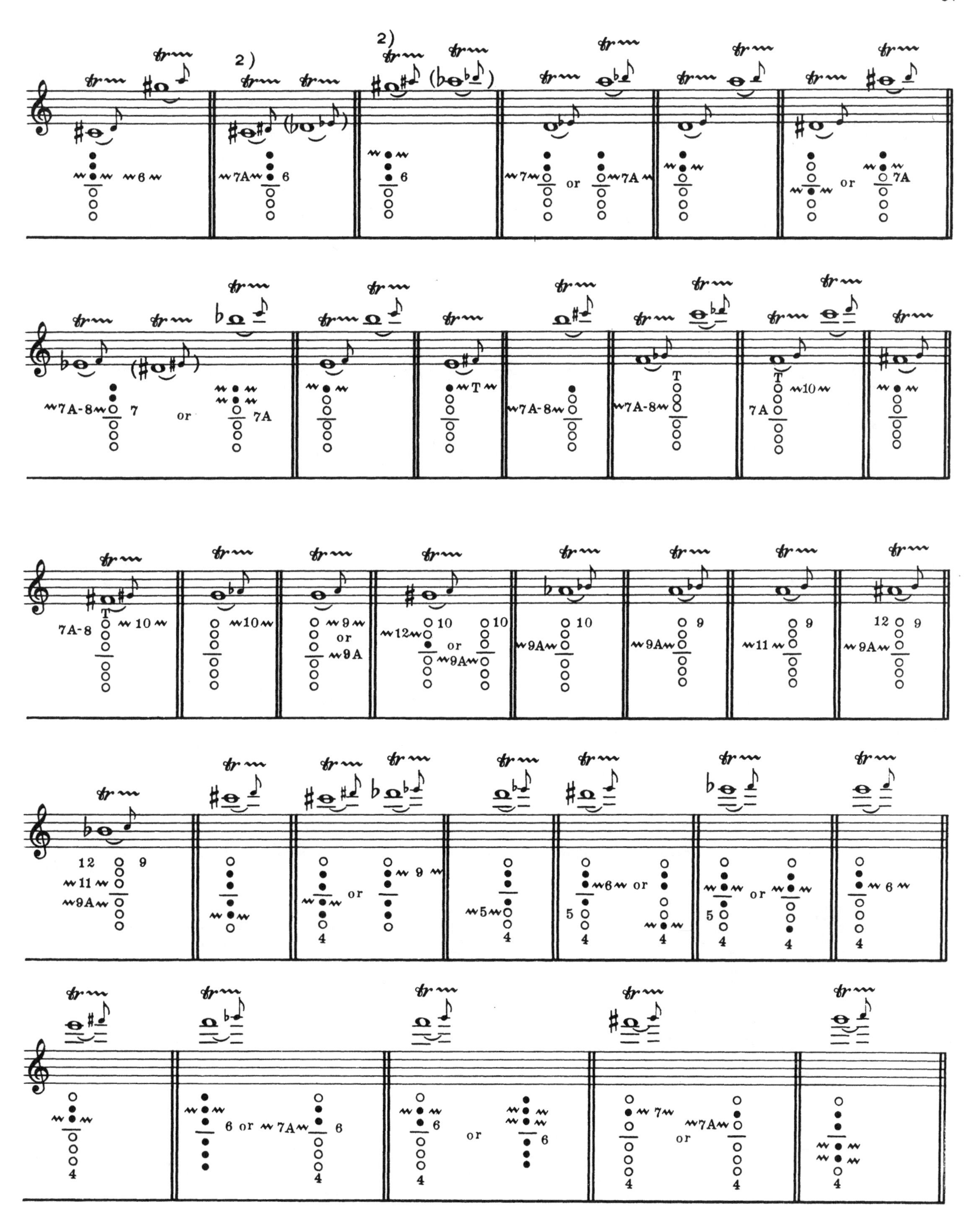

2.) Trill 6 on clarinets with forked Eb- Bb.

Musical Ornamentation (Embellishments)

Allegretto ARBAN

4

p

Moderato MAGNANI

5

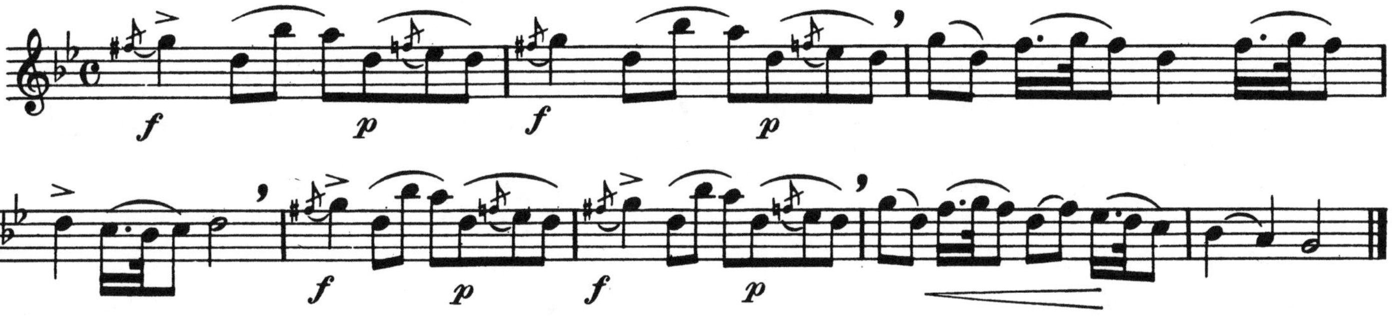

f p f p

f p f p

Andantino KLOSÉ

6

Allegretto
7
mp
p
Tempo di Mazurka
KÖHLER
8
tr

Long Grace Notes (Appoggiatura)

The Turn (Gruppetto)

In the music of Wagner it is sometimes necessary to play turns that begin on the lower instead of the upper note. The symbol for this turn is ∽.

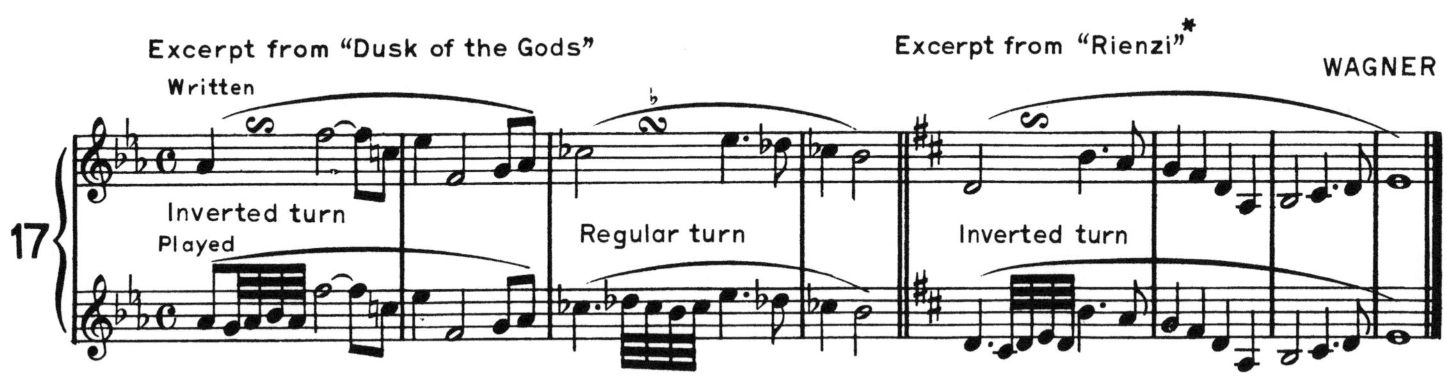

* Wagner wrote ∾ but it is traditionally played ∽.

In figures like the trill is generally executed or, sometimes,

In the music of the time of Bach and Handel (1685-1759), cadences frequently contain the figure or . The time value of the dot is not trilled, the execution being , etc. It should be added that most trills of this period should begin with the upper note, but this practice is not always observed.

Saraband

CORRETTE

In a stately manner

TELEMANN
Slowly and sustained
20
p
mf
p
mf
tr
p
rit.
Allegro moderato
KLOSÉ
21
p leggiero
mf
Fine
D.C. al Fine

22
(9)
23
f
p
f
dim.
f
24
Andante
PAUDERT
25
p dolce
tr
f
dolce

p
a tempo
PAUDERT
Andante (in six)
26
p dolce
f
mf
p
mf
p
dolce
leggiero
f
f
cadenza
p
dim.
pp
ppp

SOLOS

Variations Sentimentales

C. BAERMANN

Var. II
grazioso
più f
f
cresc.
p
rall.
a tempo
cresc.
f
Var. III
7
scherzando
segue

Caprice No. 14

FIORILLO

Gavotte and Variations

PACHELBEL

Menuetto

from Sonatina No. 3

SCHUBERT
Op. 137, No. 3

Allegro vivace

4

f p f p f p p cresc. f p ff

Fine

TRIO

p dolce

mf

pp

Menuetto da capo

Walther's Prize Song

from "Die Meistersinger"

Promenade

MARC DELMAS

Fantasy-Piece

SCHUMANN
Op.73, No.2

Lebhaft, leicht (♩=138)
(Vivace, leggiero)

7

p pp p pp p f p sfp f 1 1 1 p f sfp f p 3 3 3 3 3

segue

p
pp
p
f
1
p
pp
1
p
f
p
sfp
f
p
dolce
CODA
Nach und nach ruhiger
(a poco a poco più tranquillo)
dim.
dim.
1